# Dogs Can Say The Funniest Things in the Broad Open Daylight

Pearce W. Hammond

*LaughALot Press*
*Okatie, South Carolina*

©2014 Pearce W. Hammond

ISBN-13: 978-1497522527

ISBN-10: 1497522528

All rights reserved. No part of this book may be reproduced, stored in a retrieval system, or transmitted in any form or by any means, electronic, mechanical, digital, photocopy, recording, or any other except for brief quotations in printed reviews, without the prior permission of the author.

Printed in the United States of America

LaughALot Press
20 Bellinger Cove
Okatie, South Carolina 29909

To order additional copies of this book for family, friends and/or colleagues, log on to:

https://www.createspace.com/4742383

This book is dedicated to the memory of my two Golden Retrievers, Holly and Lorrie, who touched my life in so many ways and made this work possible.

# Man's Best Friend

We are the one absolutely unselfish friend that you can have in this selfish world. We are the one who never deserts you. We are the one that never proves ungrateful or treacherous. We are the one who will stand by you in prosperity and in poverty, in sickness and in health. We will sleep on the cold ground where the wintry winds blow and the snow drives fiercely, so we can be near your side. We will kiss the hand that has no food to offer and we will lick the wounds and sores that come in encounter with the roughness of the world. We will treat you like a prince even if you are a pauper, and when all other friends desert you, we will remain. When riches fly away and your reputation falls to pieces, we will be as constant in our love as the sun in its journey through the heavens.

> Dogs Can Say The Funniest Things in the Broad Open Daylight

# Rolling on dead birds makes the best perfume.

> Dogs Can Say The Funniest Things in the Broad Open Daylight

# Never leave home without your bone.

> Dogs Can Say The Funniest Things in the Broad Open Daylight

# Cats shouldn't have 8 more lives than dogs.

> Dogs Can Say The Funniest Things in the Broad Open Daylight

# Food always tastes better on the floor.

Dogs Can Say The Funniest Things in the Broad Open Daylight

# Happiness is a Peanut Butter covered chewstick.

| Dogs Can Say The Funniest Things in the Broad Open Daylight |
|---|

# Life is empty without a bone.

> Dogs Can Say The Funniest Things in the Broad Open Daylight

# See and hear twice as much as you bark.

Dogs Can Say The Funniest Things in the Broad Open Daylight

# Tennis balls are for mouths and not rackets.

> Dogs Can Say The Funniest Things in the Broad Open Daylight

# No dog should have to go through life without sunglasses.

> Dogs Can Say The Funniest Things in the Broad Open Daylight

# Car windows are for sticking your head out of.

> Dogs Can Say The Funniest Things in the Broad Open Daylight

# Smoked pig ears are gifts from God.

| Dogs Can Say The Funniest Things in the Broad Open Daylight |
|---|

Never trust a cat.

> Dogs Can Say The Funniest Things in the Broad Open Daylight

When you age 7 times faster than people, you deserve more respect.

> Dogs Can Say The Funniest Things in
> the Broad Open Daylight

# Always empty your bladder before leaving a Fireplug.

| Dogs Can Say The Funniest Things in the Broad Open Daylight |
|---|

# Sleeping 22 hours a day doesn't mean you are brain dead.

| Dogs Can Say The Funniest Things in the Broad Open Daylight |

True love is a slice
of Pizza you find
on the floor.

> Dogs Can Say The Funniest Things in the Broad Open Daylight

# Relief is spelled FIREPLUG.

> Dogs Can Say The Funniest Things in the Broad Open Daylight

# I'd walk a mile for a Pig Ear.

| Dogs Can Say The Funniest Things in the Broad Open Daylight |
|---|

# The best perfume comes from rolling on top of dead birds.

| Dogs Can Say The Funniest Things in the Broad Open Daylight |
|---|

# Be generous and give blood to a tick and shelter to a flea.

> Dogs Can Say The Funniest Things in
> the Broad Open Daylight

# Bark when you feel like it.

> Dogs Can Say The Funniest Things in
> the Broad Open Daylight

# Consider who will inherit your bones when you die.

| Dogs Can Say The Funniest Things in the Broad Open Daylight |
|---|

"Woofing" is the art of swallowing without tasting.

| Dogs Can Say The Funniest Things in the Broad Open Daylight |
|---|

# Shrimp breath is never caused from eating Shrimp.

| Dogs Can Say The Funniest Things in the Broad Open Daylight |

# Never criticize anyone for chasing their tail.

> Dogs Can Say The Funniest Things in the Broad Open Daylight

# Bitches and Bones are a winning combination.

| Dogs Can Say The Funniest Things in the Broad Open Daylight |
|---|

# Always have clear title to your back yard.

| Dogs Can Say The Funniest Things in the Broad Open Daylight |

Never trust your ball to a stranger.

| Dogs Can Say The Funniest Things in the Broad Open Daylight |
|---|

# Always think through your nose.

> Dogs Can Say The Funniest Things in the Broad Open Daylight

# A bitch in heat is music to your nose.

Dogs Can Say The Funniest Things in the Broad Open Daylight

# Mud puddles are the best grooming parlors.

| Dogs Can Say The Funniest Things in the Broad Open Daylight |
|---|

Always raise your tail in the company of strangers.

> Dogs Can Say The Funniest Things in the Broad Open Daylight

# Never bite the hand that treats you.

| Dogs Can Say The Funniest Things in the Broad Open Daylight |

# Sniffing butts beats kissing any day.

| Dogs Can Say The Funniest Things in the Broad Open Daylight |
|---|

# Living room sofas are more comfortable than dog houses.

| Dogs Can Say The Funniest Things in the Broad Open Daylight |
|---|

# Every dog house should have a sofa and air conditioning.

| Dogs Can Say The Funniest Things in the Broad Open Daylight |

# If your water bowl stays empty for 3 days, you've been mistaken for a Camel.

Dogs Can Say The Funniest Things in the Broad Open Daylight

# Barking keeps your throat muscles in shape.

> Dogs Can Say The Funniest Things in the Broad Open Daylight

# Noses are for finding something rotten to roll on.

| Dogs Can Say The Funniest Things in the Broad Open Daylight |
|---|

# Flea collars won't keep fleas off your rear end.

| Dogs Can Say The Funniest Things in the Broad Open Daylight |
|---|

# Brush your teeth with Chewsticks.

Dogs Can Say The Funniest Things in the Broad Open Daylight

# A T-Bone Steak a day keeps the Vet away.

| Dogs Can Say The Funniest Things in the Broad Open Daylight |
|---|

# Cars shouldn't be named after Cats.

| Dogs Can Say The Funniest Things in the Broad Open Daylight |
|---|

Never wait for your bone to come in, go out and dig it up.

| Dogs Can Say The Funniest Things in the Broad Open Daylight |
|---|

# Peanut Butter Chewsticks would change the world.

> Dogs Can Say The Funniest Things in
> the Broad Open Daylight

# Always spin around at least 4 times before eating.

| Dogs Can Say The Funniest Things in the Broad Open Daylight |

# Garbage cans are made to be turned over.

Dogs Can Say The Funniest Things in the Broad Open Daylight

# Garbage men and Mail men make my day.

| Dogs Can Say The Funniest Things in the Broad Open Daylight |

Getting a driver's license shouldn't be based on the number of legs you have.

Dogs Can Say The Funniest Things in the Broad Open Daylight

Being a 57 variety is the spice of life.

| Dogs Can Say The Funniest Things in the Broad Open Daylight |
|---|

The 5 most important words in any language are:

*The Pizza Man is Coming.*

> Dogs Can Say The Funniest Things in the Broad Open Daylight

# Always eat the Pizza before the kids get home from school.

> Dogs Can Say The Funniest Things in the Broad Open Daylight

# Never roll on top of anything that smells good.

> Dogs Can Say The Funniest Things in the Broad Open Daylight

# Water tastes much better out of a toilet.

| Dogs Can Say The Funniest Things in the Broad Open Daylight |
|---|

# A day without meat is like a day without sunshine.

> Dogs Can Say The Funniest Things in the Broad Open Daylight

# Happiness is keeping your nose in the dirt.

| Dogs Can Say The Funniest Things in the Broad Open Daylight |
|---|

# Never lie down without scratching the ground.

> Dogs Can Say The Funniest Things in the Broad Open Daylight

Always crap on a lawn when the homeowner is watching.

| Dogs Can Say The Funniest Things in the Broad Open Daylight |

# What stays on the kitchen counter is yours and what hits the floor is mine.

> Dogs Can Say The Funniest Things in the Broad Open Daylight

# Any pill the Vet gives you should be buried inside of a pound of Peanut Butter.

> Dogs Can Say The Funniest Things in the Broad Open Daylight

# Chasing cars should become an Olympic Event.

| Dogs Can Say The Funniest Things in the Broad Open Daylight |
|---|

A double Cheeseburger a day keeps the Vet away.

| Dogs Can Say The Funniest Things in the Broad Open Daylight |

Mail men make the hair stand up on your back.

| Dogs Can Say The Funniest Things in the Broad Open Daylight |
|---|

# Road kill always makes its own gravy.

> Dogs Can Say The Funniest Things in the Broad Open Daylight

# 4 legs are better than 2.

| Dogs Can Say The Funniest Things in the Broad Open Daylight |
|---|

# Real Bar-B-Que is a smoked Pig Ear.

# The Bill of Rights for Dogs

If we like it, it's ours.

If it's in our mouth, it's ours.

If we can take it from you, it's ours.

If we had it a little while ago, it's ours.

If it's ours, it must never be yours in any way.

If we're chewing something up, all the pieces are ours.

If it just looks like ours, it's ours.

If we saw it first, it's ours.

If you are playing with something and put it down, it automatically becomes ours.

If it's broken, it's ours.

# About The Author

Pearce W. Hammond was born and raised in Savannah, Georgia and has been a dog owner and dog lover most of his life. His writing skills came to him quite honestly and are in his blood. His great uncle was famed Savannah, Georgia-born songwriter, Johnny Mercer, who wrote over 1,000 songs and won four Academy Awards.

In addition to this book, Mr. Hammond has written several other humorous books which include *"Funnybone"* and *"Funnybone 2"* that contain hilarious jokes and quotes about age and aging and senior moments. He has also written a humorous book about frequent flying titled, *"Frequent Flying Should Only Be For Birds"* and another book about dogs titled, *"Listen To Me"*, which he says was really written by his two Golden Retrievers.

Other works include two books about the Gullah and Geechee people of South Carolina and Georgia titled, *"The Gullahs of South Carolina"* and *"Gone with the Tide."* Each book is illustrated with his original art.

He and his wife, Anne, now reside on the tidal waters of the Chechessee River in Okatie, South Carolina.

Made in the USA
San Bernardino, CA
06 January 2018